Who Am I?

&

How Shall I Live?

andrew cohen

Who Am I?

&

How Shall I Live?

Moksha Press 1998

Moksha Press Cataloging
Cohen, Andrew, 1955 Oct. 23-
Who am i? & how shall i live? / by Andrew Cohen.
p. cm.
ISBN 1-883929-24-5
1. Spiritual Life.   2. Life.   I. Title.
BL624   299.93—dc21

Foreword

I had the extraordinary experience of being in the audience when Andrew Cohen gave this talk in New Delhi, India, and each time I encounter his words, I am awestruck at the simplicity and power of this call to consciousness and conscience. If you have ever longed for wholeness, felt the call of the heart or simply wanted this insane world to be different, you'll be surprised, and even relieved, at the possibility for the depth of humanity that is revealed here. Andrew makes the path to absolute transformation perfectly real, perfectly clear and perfectly practical.

How can I describe what happened on that night in New Delhi? I sat down at the back of an auditorium filled with the sensuous chaos of India—passionate conversation rising and falling, people jostling for space, a subtle cacophony of colors and styles of dress, music pounding from a nearby party, the scent of flowers. I was intensely curious how Andrew would respond to a primarily Indian audience who was almost wholly unfamiliar with his teaching, and I was shocked when, in his first few words, he boldly declared that he was going to present *everything anyone needed to know to lead an enlightened life!* And yet in the next hour and a half, this is exactly what he did. With a logic so blinding in its clarity that it almost eluded the mind, Andrew placed the entire universe, and our place within it, before us. Speaking about meditation and contemplation within the context of the two fundamental questions of spiritual life—*Who am I?* and *How shall*

I live?—he made the possibility and responsibility for true wholeness of being our own.

As Andrew spoke of the miracle of deep meditation, his words were carried on the force of a mystery greater than each of us, and yet at the same time the deepest expression of who we are. No gap existed between the words and the speaker: Andrew *was* what he was saying. The intelligence of Life itself was speaking. Through Andrew's simple but profound instructions, meditation suddenly became a revelation. Who I thought I was began to slip away. Something subtle yet palpable began to fill each of us and the space between us. What we heard became what we experienced—a possibility for human existence heretofore only imagined but now completely real. We found ourselves drowning in the infinite depths of our truest Self.

Stressing the absolute importance of contemplation in spiritual life, Andrew introduced five fundamental tenets of Enlightenment. With these five tenets, he laid out a psychology of truth to guide us in action. These tenets have the power to harness the mind as an engine of the absolute truth of our *being*. They are so deceptively simple, so blindingly clear. They exist almost outside of comprehension. These tenets, when used as tools to inquire into what we are actually doing, penetrate through confusion and obscurity like lasers. They are unfathomably deep. I am constantly amazed that through them we can engage with *any* aspect of our humanity—from the hideous to the sublime—and find that *everything begins to make sense!* As Andrew spoke of these five tenets, I found that something profound began to fall into alignment at the core of my being. Something finally came home to rest. Yes, we are the problem, but we can *choose* to be the solution.

If you take Andrew's words seriously, you may find, as I have, that he reveals what you have always most deeply known and wanted more than anything else but lacked the courage to really live, or just didn't believe was possible in the world as it is. He shows us the way to the deepest integrity imaginable between *being* and *living* on this earth. Glimpsing the glory that Andrew brings to us, we are left with only one question: will we dare to find out who we really are and then *live* the truth of what we discover? The most breathtaking possibility for a true humanity is here for us to choose.

— *Elizabeth Debold*

"I'm going to go into great depth in this talk about everything that any sincere human being needs to know if they want to be free. I know this is quite a bold declaration, but I'm sure that by the end of the talk at least some people will recognize that what I'm saying is actually true."

Part 1

The heart of the spiritual life ultimately consists of two fundamental experiences: *meditation* and *contemplation*.

Meditation is the experience of *being*. When we experience meditation—whether we are practicing it or simply experiencing the spontaneous flow of meditation within ourselves—meditation is the experience of *being* beyond the mind. The experience of meditation, when it is spontaneous, effortless and deep, is often quite a revelation. Indeed, when we are able to experience who and what we are outside of and beyond the movement of the mind, we discover a depth of self that is profound. And in those moments we experience a dynamic freedom from everything that we have ever known. You see, most of the time we are mechanically identifying with one thought after another, and because of that our emotional experience is often one of suffocation and limitation. But when we experience consciousness free from the movement of mind, it is always the experience of extraordinary liberation.

Contemplation is the pursuit of *truth*. The pursuit of truth means that the individual endeavors to find out for themselves: what is the difference between *truth* and *falsehood?* If we look around at the world we live in, we will find that it is a very rare individual who is interested in what is true. In fact, most of us simply assume that we already know. We have all absorbed countless unquestioned ideas from the world around us and from the culture that we live in. And it takes tremendous courage and a rare intensity of interest to be able to *independently* question ideas that we already have in order to find out directly for ourselves what is true.

So in the experience of meditation, we leave the mind alone. We allow ourselves to experience *being,* free from the influence of thought. While in the practice of contemplation, which is the intense, focused, one-pointed pursuit of truth, we *do* use the mind. In contemplation we use thought in order to help us discriminate between truth and falsehood.

But in order to be able to practice the art of contemplation, the art of discrimination, first we have to learn how to meditate. First we have to learn how to experience being beyond the mind. It's very difficult to practice the art of contemplation if we have not yet discovered that infinite space that lies beyond the mind.

Meditation
Letting Everything Be as It Is

The most direct way to experience meditation is simply to *let everything be as it is*. Just let everything be as it is—over and over and over again.

Now the minute we try to let everything be as it is, what we discover is that *we don't want to do it*. And the reason for this is that we are so compulsively fascinated with the contents of our own mind—our likes, our dislikes and all of our worries. And because of this, our mind, when we begin to look closely at it, often *appears* to be tormenting us. But if we want to be free we will find the strength to be disinterested in the contents of our own mind. If we want to be free we will find the courage to simply *let everything be as it is.* You see, to let everything be as it is, all we have to do is resist the temptation *not* to let everything be as it is. This is the great challenge that the meditator struggles with.

Of course there are different approaches to meditation. Some approaches are meant to help distract us from the movement of the mind. But if we want to look very deeply into life, we shouldn't distract ourselves. We should simply let everything be as it is. And as we let everything be as it is and continue to let everything be as it is, the mind will begin to slow down. It will fall away from the center of consciousness and we will discover *space.* Infinite space. And in that space there is depth, extraordinary depth. And in that depth we will discover peace, bliss and joy because finally *we want nothing*.

When the mind is busy we always want something. It's an endless torment. But when the mind moves away from the center of consciousness we begin to feel the intense peace of *letting everything be as it is*. And when we experience this very deep peace, we discover the secret of Enlightenment. It's the secret that the Buddha was speaking about. We find our greatest happiness, greatest joy and deepest fulfillment *when we want nothing*.

Most of us live a life of almost unending tyranny. And that tyranny is caused by the presence of ceaseless wanting. The truth is, there is no object that we can possess in this world that can give us lasting peace and perfect contentment. It simply does not exist. And only when we experience very deep meditation, *which is the conscious experience of wanting nothing,* will this perennial truth begin to dawn. If we are serious, eventually it will become unavoidably clear that the fundamental cause of our misery is the constant seeking for contentment outside of ourselves. So the ultimate act of renunciation, which is the direct path to Liberation, is simply the willingness to give up this endless seeking for gratification outside of our own self. This is the secret of Enlightenment, and it can be discovered through the deep and profound experience of meditation.

Now as I said, in order to practice contemplation we first need to be able to experience very deep and profound meditation. Because in order to learn how to use the mind in the right way, we have to first be able to put the mind down. You see, most of us are so compulsively distracted by the movement of mind that *the mind and its movement is all that we see.* And when the movement of mind is all that we see, it will be impossible for us to have any *objectivity* in relationship to that movement. It is the discovery of the SPACE that we experience in meditation that makes it possible to see the mind from *outside* the mind, to see the mind from *beyond* the mind. The experiential discovery of that space reveals a completely new perspective in relationship to the mind and its movement that is liberatingly *objective* instead of suffocatingly *subjective.*

Once we become firmly established in the experience of meditation—when we know what it is to leave the mind alone, *to let everything be as it is*—then and only then can we begin to use the mind with an objectivity that is profound, an objectivity that will enable us to see what is true.

Part 2

There are two fundamental spiritual questions: *Who am I?* and *How shall I live?* To find the answer to the first question, we ask the universe: "Who am I? Who am I *really?* Who am I beyond the mind, beyond the personality, beyond gender, beyond *any fixed notion of self?—Who am I?*"

The second question that all true seekers want to know the answer to is: "*How shall I live?* How can I live in a way that makes perfect sense? How can I live in a way that manifests the spiritual vision of profound simplicity, dynamic freedom and perfect oneness?" All the questions that have been asked of spiritual masters throughout history in the end refer to these two questions alone: *Who am I?* and *How shall I live?*

The answer to the first question is found in deep meditation, where we can experience who we are beyond the mind, beyond the personality. And when we have a repeated experiential discovery of who we are beyond the mind—who we are when we want nothing, when we need nothing, when we know nothing—suddenly or gradually a conviction is born. A conviction that whispers—*"Yes. This is who I really am."*

The second spiritual question becomes relevant when our experience of meditation comes to an end. When we've experienced the peace, joy, bliss and absolute contentment of wanting nothing at all, and then the world in all its unrelenting intensity suddenly rushes in—*what are we going to do?* You see, as long as we are breathing we must ACT. There is no choice in this. And if we want to be free, we have to be able to respond fully and wholeheartedly to the ultimate challenge. What is that challenge? That challenge is being *liberated* in the world of time and space, being *free* in the world of cause and effect, being *enlightened* in the world of you and me. This is where the practice of contemplation comes into the spiritual life.

Contemplation
The Five Fundamental Tenets of Enlightenment

Now I'm going to speak about what in my teaching are called *The Five Fundamental Tenets of Enlightenment.* They serve as a perfect foundation for enlightened action in the world of time and space. Sincere contemplation of these five tenets will enable any seeker to find out, simply and directly, what the appropriate response to life is in any given moment if they want to be free more than anything else.

The First Tenet: *Clarity of Intention*

The first tenet, *Clarity of Intention,* states that if we want to be free, then we have to cultivate the *intention* to be free to such a degree that it will always be more powerful than *any other desire.* The first tenet tells us that if we want to succeed in liberating ourselves from fear, ignorance and self-deception, then that desire for Liberation must always be stronger than any interest in wealth or worldly fame, more powerful than even our love for our children, our husband or our wife. Simply put, the first tenet says that our desire for spiritual freedom must become *the most important thing in our lives.* Indeed, for success to be a realistic possibility, the first tenet tells us that our desire for Liberation has to be cultivated to such a degree that it *alone* becomes that which determines the choices that we make and the actions that we take.

Of course, very few of us want to be free *that* much, because it demands such unusual courage. You see, the world we live in insists that we all conform. But the individual who wants to be free more than anything else must be unwilling to conform. They must be ready to stand alone in that which they have recognized is most important.

If we sincerely want to become a liberated person, then we have to be willing to be independent in a world where so few truly think for themselves.

The Second Tenet: *The Law of Volitionality*

The second tenet, *The Law of Volitionality*, states that we are not victims of our experience. You see, most of us, secretly or even not so secretly, feel victimized *simply being alive.* The second tenet tells us that the individual who wants to be free more than anything else, who wants to be a truly independent, liberated human being, *unconditionally rejects any and all temptations to be a victim.* They unconditionally accept full responsibility for their "karma," for their lot in life, even if they have had a very hard time.

The second tenet tells us that there is only one doer and that doer is *us.* It states that it is we and we alone who are making the important choices. The second tenet tells us that if we want to be free more than anything else, we have to be willing to take responsibility for the consequences of everything that has ever happened to us. It tells us that only then does it become possible to be free from the past—*in this very moment.*

The Third Tenet: *Face Everything and Avoid Nothing*

The third tenet is very simple. It states that if we want to be free more than anything else, we have to be willing to *face everything and avoid nothing in every moment.* Facing everything and avoiding nothing is the ultimate spiritual practice. It requires tremendous courage, unusual sincerity and a powerful commitment. Most of all, facing everything and avoiding nothing in every moment demands that we have a VERY BIG HEART. Why? *Because it means that we always want to know the truth, and that we are willing to face everything and avoid nothing no matter how painful it may be, in order to find it.*

It's very important to realize that in the end, if we are not willing to face ourselves unconditionally, then there is no doubt that someone else is going to suffer as a result. This is inevitable.

Simply through this practice, the practice of facing everything and avoiding nothing, we will cease to act out of ignorance in ways that cause suffering to other people. Through this practice alone, we can find our own Liberation.

The Fourth Tenet: *The Truth of Impersonality*

The fourth tenet states that *every aspect of our personal experience is ultimately completely impersonal.* It declares that our ignorance of that fact is the cause of so much of our fear, confusion and unenlightenment. The fourth tenet tells us that there is only *one human experience,* but that everybody believes their experience to be unique to them alone.

When we step back from the compulsive and habitual *personalization* of our own experience, it will become shockingly apparent to us that none of what we experience is ultimately personal. For example, when two different individuals experience the peace, joy and bliss of wanting nothing at all, aren't they experiencing the *very same* peace, joy and bliss? Similarly, when two different individuals experience fear, anger and lust, in the end aren't they experiencing the very same fear, the very same anger and the very same lust?

The fourth tenet says that when we are willing to resist the seemingly overwhelming temptation to personalize almost everything that we experience, we will begin to become aware of the universal nature of our experience, the universal nature of human consciousness. Who will we be when we no longer habitually and compulsively personalize our own experience? If we want to be free more than anything else, that's what we want to discover.

You see, one of the greatest causes of human ignorance, and the relentless suffering and agony that is its result, is the compulsive and habitual personalization of that which is not personal but universal.

The Fifth Tenet: *For the Sake of the Whole*

The last tenet of the teaching is the most demanding of all. It states that to be a truly free human being we have to give up our materialistic relationship to life. A materialistic relationship to life is defined as a life lived only for ourselves. It is a life where we are living only to *have* for ourselves, only to *get* for ourselves. Even Enlightenment *we want for ourselves alone.*

The last tenet states that if we want to be a liberated human being, we must come to that point in our own evolution where we are no longer living for ourselves but are living *for the sake of the whole.* It tells us that genuine spirituality always points to the end of a self-centered, self-serving relationship to life. It makes clear that the sincere spiritual aspirant must be willing to give up this terrible habit of living for themselves *alone*. This is the last step that needs to be taken by any human being who truly wants to be free.

All human beings want to be free from suffering, all human beings want to be free from fear. But there is more to the spiritual life than that. You see, the point of spiritual experience, in fact the whole point of Enlightenment, is *evolution*. The evolution of consciousness. And this evolution occurs when we recognize in a way that is unequivocal that *the whole point of human life is to live for the sake of the whole*. When we realize this we experience intense bliss, because in this realization there is final Liberation. The most significant part of spiritual experience is the discovery of why we are here. And when we discover that the whole point of human existence is to live for the sake of the whole, *all of our questions are answered.*

This is the hardest of the tenets. And that is because it demands *everything* from us. But it is where true Liberation is found.

Once again, the first tenet is *Clarity of Intention.* It states that if one sincerely aspires to achieve Liberation and Enlightenment in this life, then the desire for that Liberation must be cultivated in such a way that it will *always* be stronger than our desire for anything else.

The second tenet is *The Law of Volitionality.* It states that there is only one doer and that that doer is *us.* It says that the unconditional acceptance of that fact makes it possible to take complete responsibility for the consequences of everything that has ever happened to us. It tells us that only then does Liberation become possible.

The third tenet is *Face Everything and Avoid Nothing.* It states simply that if we want to be free, we have to be willing to face everything and avoid nothing in every moment. It says that if we are not willing to face everything and avoid nothing, then it is inevitable that others will suffer the consequences of our own unwillingness to be awake. It tells us that facing everything and avoiding nothing is the ultimate spiritual practice, and that if we want to be free our Liberation depends upon it.

The fourth tenet is *The Truth of Impersonality.* It states that every aspect of our personal experience, when scrutinized closely enough, will be revealed to be completely *impersonal.* It says that the discovery of the ultimately impersonal nature of our personal experience is the door to direct perception of the universal nature of *all* human experience. It tells us that it is through the direct perception of the universal nature of our own experience that the truth can be known.

The fifth and final tenet is *For the Sake of the Whole.* It states that to be truly free we must finally be willing to renounce a relationship to life that is based on wanting to have everything, *including spiritual experience*, for ourselves alone. It says that the whole point of spiritual experience is evolution. And it tells us that that evolution occurs, and the true significance of human life is found, when we cease to live for ourselves but live only for the sake of the whole.

Through the sincere contemplation of these five tenets, the way to actually *live* the enlightened vision—the vision of nonduality—is revealed.

The End of Duality

As I said, the heart of the spiritual life ultimately consists of two fundamental experiences: *meditation* and *contemplation.*

In the experience of deep meditation, we discover who we are beyond the mind. And it is in that discovery that we find the answer to the question, *Who am I?* The answer is found by giving up all temptation to struggle, by letting *absolutely everything* be as it is. Through simply letting everything be as it is, we will experience SPACE—a vast, expansive emptiness where there is deep, deep peace. This is a place where nothing ever happened, a place before the universe was born. When we experience that miraculous depth inside our own self, we recognize who we really are. In this state of deep and profound peace, we experience our True Self.

In the practice of contemplation, we deliberately use the mind to find the answer to the question, *How shall I live?* We deliberately and intentionally use the mind in order to be true to the depth of Self that we have discovered. When we ask the question, *How shall I live?*, we want to know *how to be true to our True Self*, how to be true to the peace, joy, bliss and perfect contentment that we found in the experience of deep meditation. If we are sincere, we want there to be no contradiction between the Self that we experience in meditation and the self that we are as an individual human being who acts and reacts in the world of time and space. In a liberated individual these two different experiences of self merge and become one.

Spiritual practice done in earnest can bring us to a place where the life that we live, the very *human* life that we live, is free from fundamental contradiction, a place where our own personality becomes a clear expression of that perfect peace that lies deep within us.

Biography

Andrew Cohen *is not just a spiritual teacher—he is an inspiring phenomenon. Since his awakening in 1986 he has only lived, breathed and spoken of one thing: the potential of total liberation from the bondage of ignorance, superstition and self-ishness. Powerless to limit his unceasing investigation, he has looked at the "jewel of enlightenment" from every angle, and given birth to a teaching that is vast and subtle, yet incomparably direct and revolutionary in its impact.*

Through his public teachings, his books and his meetings with spiritual leaders of almost every tradition, he has tirelessly sought to convey his discovery that spiritual liberation's true significance is its potential to completely transform not only the individual, but the entire way that human beings, as a race, live together. In sharp contrast to the cynicism which is so pervasive today, yet with full awareness of the difficult challenges that we face, he has dared to teach and to show that it is indeed possible to bring heaven to earth. This powerful message of unity, openness and love has inspired many who have heard it to join together to prove its reality with their own lives, igniting an ever expanding international revolution of tremendous vitality and significance.

OTHER BOOKS BY ANDREW COHEN

Freedom Has No History
Enlightenment Is a Secret
An Unconditional Relationship to Life
Autobiography of an Awakening
My Master Is My Self
The Promise of Perfection
An Absolute Relationship to Life
The Challenge of Enlightenment

IMPERSONAL ENLIGHTENMENT FELLOWSHIP
CENTERS FOR THE TEACHINGS OF ANDREW COHEN

Founded in 1988, Impersonal Enlightenment Fellowship is a nonprofit organization that supports and facilitates the teaching work of Andrew Cohen. It is dedicated to the enlightenment of the individual and the expression of enlightenment in the world. For more information about Andrew Cohen and his teaching, please contact:

UNITED STATES

INTERNATIONAL CENTER
P.O. Box 2360
Lenox, MA 01240
tel: 413-637-6000 or 800-376-3210
fax: 413-637-6015
email: moksha@moksha.org
website: http://www.moksha.org

BOSTON CENTER
2269 Massachusetts Avenue
Cambridge, MA 02140
tel: 617-492-2848
fax: 617-876-3525
email: 73214.602@compuserve.com

NEW YORK CENTER
311 Broadway, Suite 2A
New York, NY 10007
tel: 212-233-1930
fax: 212-233-1986
email: info@faceny.org

EUROPE

LONDON CENTER
Centre Studios
Englands Lane
London NW3 4YD UK
tel: 44-171-419-8100
fax: 44-171-419-8101
email: 100074.3662@compuserve.com
website: http://www.moksha.org/faceag.htm

AMSTERDAM CENTER
Oudeschans 46A
1011 LC Amsterdam, Holland
tel: 31-20-422-1616
fax: 31-20-422-2417
email: 100412.160@compuserve.com
website: http://www.moksha.org/face/nl

COLOGNE CENTER
Elsasstrasse 69
50677 Cologne, Germany
tel: 49-221-310-1040
fax: 49-221-331-9439
email: 100757.3605@compuserve.com

STOCKHOLM CENTER
Roslagsgatan 48nb
113 54 Stockholm, Sweden
tel: 46-8-458-9970
fax: 46-8-458-9971
email: ac.center@swipnet.se

OTHER CENTERS

SYDNEY CENTER
479 Darling Street
Balmain, Sydney
NSW 2041 Australia
tel: 61-2-9555-2932
fax: 61-2-9555-2931
email: 105312.2467@compuserve.com

RISHIKESH CENTER
PO Box 20
Sivananda Nagar, Distr. Tehri Garhwal
U.P. 249192, India
tel: 91-1-135-435-303
fax: 91-1-135-435-302
email: iefrish@nde.vsnl.net.in